I admit, I made some mistakes.

(U)ntil the 1991–92 season there really hadn't been much written or said negatively about me. After we won the first championship there wasn't anything anyone could really say about my basketball anymore so they started looking at me personally. I admit, I made some mistakes. They weren't huge mistakes, not the kind that change your life. But I also stood up and faced the fire. The gambling stories were situations I put myself in and I was responsible for my actions. But the way I dealt with those situations, particularly the gambling issue, was human. I made a mistake and I faced the heat. To some degree I think people started seeing me as more like

them, more of a person with problems and issues. The way I had been perceived up to that point really wasn't reality. It was a difficult time, but I grew up. I was no longer just playing a game that paid me a lot of money and earned me the adoration of millions of fans. It wasn't that simple anymore, and in some ways it wasn't that pure, either. I was experiencing basketball as a business, on and off the court. I didn't make any serious mistakes, I didn't have trouble with alcohol, drugs, or anything like that, but I wasn't some kind of perfect person that floated above life's day-to-day issues.

second

THE 1992 FINALS AGAINST PORTLAND WERE SUPPOSED TO DETERMINE

THE DIFFERENCE BETWEEN CLYDE DREXLER AND MYSELF.

To that point Clyde had been seen as a version of me, not necessarily a better version. So I'm sure that presented a challenge for him. But I took that discussion the same way. I wanted people to know there was a distinct difference, just as there was when I played against Magic, Charles, and other big-name players. I used the first championship against Magic to gain credibility. He was the guy on top at the time and I had to beat him to earn my place. By the time we played Portland I was the guy on top because we were the defending champions. Clyde wanted to use me the same way I used Magic. Later in my career, players wanted to go through the Chicago Bulls because it would legitimize the championship. I thought there was a difference, a real difference. It was similar to the 1998 All-Star game when Kobe Bryant was

1992 NBA FINALS COMPARISON		
JORDAN		**CLYDE**
6	G	6
254	MIN	238
154	FGA	118
81	FGM	48
46	FTA	56
41	FTM	50
29	RB	47
39	AST	32
10	STL	8
2	BLK	6
215	PTS	149
35.8	AVG	24.8
46	HI	32

trying to make his mark against me. It's not something you announce but it's a challenge that simmers right below the surface. I was trying to break Clyde down by using all the facets of my game to say, "Don't even think about it." Besides, I had studied Clyde. I knew that if he hit his first three shots there wasn't a shot on the floor he wouldn't take. Interestingly, he was more dangerous if he missed the first three because he would focus on other aspects of the game. He would look to go to the basket and pick up a foul. He did have that great first step. I'm pretty sure he tried to push me to my left as well because that was my weaker hand. Portland played us tough but repeating was never about the physical difficulty involved in getting the job done. Winning two or three titles in a row was always more mental than physical. The only exception to that notion was 1998, which was a very physically draining year with all the injuries and the lack of understanding by some players about what it took to win three straight.

IF THERE IS ONE PLAYER I WOULD HAVE LIKED TO PLAY AGAINST IN HIS PRIME IT WOULD HAVE BEEN

Jerry West.

	Jerry WEST	Michael JORDAN
SEASONS		
	14	13
ALL-NBA FIRST TEAM		
	10	10
ALL-DEFENSIVE FIRST TEAM*		
	4	9
MOST VALUABLE PLAYER		
	0	5
SCORING AVERAGE		
	27.0	31.5
ALL-STAR GAMES		
	14	12
FG PERCENTAGES		
	.474	.505
FT PERCENTAGES		
	.814	.838
REBOUNDS		
	5.8	6.3
ASSISTS		
	6.7	5.4
PLAYOFF SCORING AVERAGES		
	29.1	33.4

*Team started in 1968-69, West's 9th season

He was a great clutch shooter, he could jump, he was tough, and he was quick.
I would have liked to test myself against him at his best.

HOW WOULD I HAVE DONE?

We'll never know. From what I have read about Jerry and from what others have told me,
he played the game a lot like I did. He was a great scorer, but he also played good defense.
Could he have stopped me? I don't think so.

COULD I HAVE STOPPED HIM?

I don't know. But it would have been a great matchup.

It might sound strange, but I've often wondered how I would have done against myself.
How would I have attacked at the offensive end? What would I have done defensively? There were some cracks, but I'm never going to tell anybody what they were. I think I could have done some things defensively, but I also know I would have come up with ways to counter those tactics offensively. The difference would have been mental. I wouldn't be able to out-think myself. The heart would be the same, the work ethic just as strong. I wouldn't have had an edge, at least not the edge I had against everyone else. Some nights it was being smarter, some nights stronger, and some nights just tougher. I could jump over certain guys, get by others, and later take most of them into the post. If I couldn't throw off their rhythm defensively, then I would attack them at the offensive end. I felt like I had a lot of weapons and not all of them were physical in nature. But against myself? I know myself too well. I can't say I would have won because that means I would have lost. It would have been fun to watch, though.

THE NEW YORK KNICKS TEAMS OF THE EARLY 1970S WERE VERY SIMILAR IN MAKEUP TO OUR FIRST THREE CHAMPIONSHIP TEAMS. EVEN THE COACHES, RED HOLZMAN AND PHIL, WERE SIMILAR IN THE WAY THEY FOCUSED ON TEAM DEFENSE AND DEALT WITH PLAYERS. THE KNICKS HAD WILLIS REED, DAVE DEBUSSCHERE, BILL BRADLEY, AND WALT FRAZIER. BOTH TEAMS DISTRIBUTED THE BALL SELFLESSLY AND WORKED AS A UNIT TO MAKE THINGS HAPPEN AT THE DEFENSIVE END. WE HAD BILL CARTWRIGHT, JOHN PAXSON, SCOTTIE, AND ME. THE FIRST TWO CHAMPIONSHIP SEASONS WE WERE CONNECTED JUST LIKE THOSE KNICKS TEAMS. BILL WAS LIKE REED, PAXSON WAS SMART LIKE BRADLEY, PIPPEN DID A LITTLE OF EVERYTHING LIKE DEBUSSCHERE, AND I PLAYED BOTH ENDS LIKE FRAZIER. LIKE OUR BULLS TEAMS, THOSE KNICKS COULD HAVE WON IN ANY ERA. THE GAME MAY CHANGE AND PLAYERS MAY BECOME

DAVE DEBUSSCHERE   WALT FRAZIER   WILLIS REED   PHIL JACKSON   BILL BRADLEY

MORE SKILLED, BUT THE KIND OF PLAYERS WHO WIN CHAMPI- ONSHIPS NEVER CHANGE. GIVE ME GUYS WITH HEART, BRAINS, AND STRONG FUNDAMENTALS. NO MATTER WHAT HAPPENS IN THE GAME OF BASKETBALL, THOSE ELEMENTS WILL ALWAYS DETERMINE SUC- CESS AND FAILURE. LOOK AROUND THE NBA. WERE THE BULLS ALWAYS THE MOST TALENTED TEAM? NEVER. OUR LAST THREE CHAM- PIONSHIP TEAMS WERE HELD TOGETHER BY A COMMON BOND. WE KNEW HOW TO PLAY THE GAME AND WE KNEW HOW TO WIN. INDIVIDUAL ABILITY PUT US IN POSITION, BUT EVERYTHING ELSE IS WHAT PUT US OVER THE TOP. JUST LIKE THOSE KNICKS TEAMS, WE HAD LEARNED HOW TO BREAK DOWN AN OPPONENT AND EXECUTE WHEN THE GAME WAS ON THE LINE. THAT'S HEART. AND THAT COMES FROM WITHIN. GIVE ME FOUR GUYS WITH GREAT HEART AND I'LL BEAT FIVE GUYS WITH GREAT POTENTIAL ANY TIME.

STACEY KING   WILL PERDUE   BILL CARTWRIGHT   SCOTT WILLIAMS
B.J. ARMSTRONG   SCOTTIE PIPPEN   HORACE GRANT   JOHN PAXSON

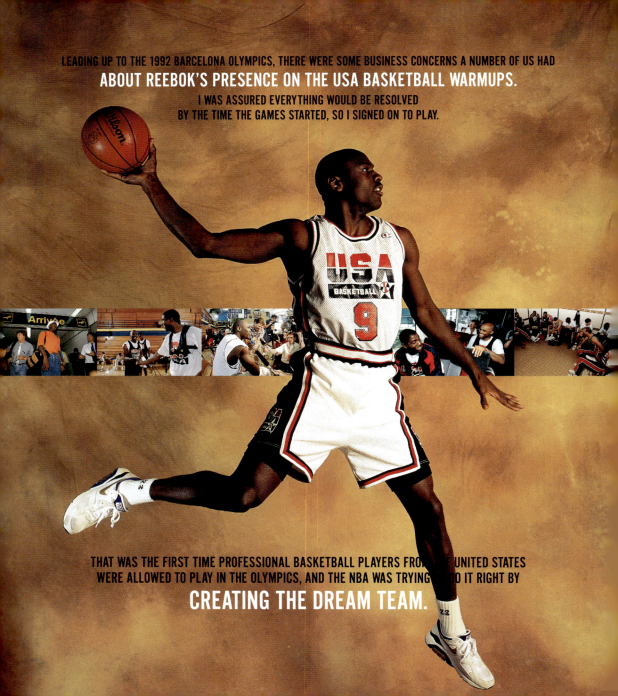

LEADING UP TO THE 1992 BARCELONA OLYMPICS, THERE WERE SOME BUSINESS CONCERNS A NUMBER OF US HAD
ABOUT REEBOK'S PRESENCE ON THE USA BASKETBALL WARMUPS.
I WAS ASSURED EVERYTHING WOULD BE RESOLVED
BY THE TIME THE GAMES STARTED, SO I SIGNED ON TO PLAY.

THAT WAS THE FIRST TIME PROFESSIONAL BASKETBALL PLAYERS FROM THE UNITED STATES
WERE ALLOWED TO PLAY IN THE OLYMPICS, AND THE NBA WAS TRYING TO DO IT RIGHT BY
CREATING THE DREAM TEAM.

I HAD WON A GOLD MEDAL IN THE 1984 GAMES,
SO MY FIRST THOUGHT WAS TO ALLOW SOMEONE ELSE TO HAVE THE OPPORTUNITY.

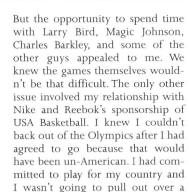

But the opportunity to spend time with Larry Bird, Magic Johnson, Charles Barkley, and some of the other guys appealed to me. We knew the games themselves wouldn't be that difficult. The only other issue involved my relationship with Nike and Reebok's sponsorship of USA Basketball. I knew I couldn't back out of the Olympics after I had agreed to go because that would have been un-American. I had committed to play for my country and I wasn't going to pull out over a

logo, despite my loyalties. Still, I didn't know how I would handle the medal ceremony. I wasn't about to stand up there in front of the world wearing a Reebok product. When it came time to receive the gold medal, we were told anyone who refused to wear the warmup wouldn't be allowed on the stand. Finally, about 20 minutes before the medal ceremony, I came up with an idea. Charles Barkley, Scottie Pippen, and I decided to go into the stands and collect American flags.

WHO COULD ARGUE WITH THE FLAG?
WE GOT ONLY FOUR OF THEM, BUT EACH OF US DRAPED ONE OVER THE LOGO.

We might have been just as successful if Phil had been more of a company man, but I don't think our chemistry would have been as good. We wouldn't have felt the same level of obligation. I'm not sure some of the other players would have gone that extra mile. Phil dealt with us every day and he understood what our objectives were as a unit. He understood, from one day to the next, what was happening with us individually and collectively. He was the only one who knew. No one else in the organization had that kind of insight. How could they?

Phil knew our strengths, he knew our weaknesses. Theoretically, if you had a dispute with the coach, a player or that player's agent could go to management and complain. But we had no dispute with Phil because we knew his primary objective was to put together the best team. We all had the same objective, and Phil knew more about the individual parts than anyone.

Guys like Jud Buechler relied upon Jerry Krause for a contract, so they had to stay in Jerry's good graces. But those guys also relied on me, Scottie, and Phil. I had a voice and I had options, so players kind of lived through me when it came to dealing with management. I never minced words with Jerry. I let him know exactly how I felt right to his face.

As players, we drew a line between the team and the rest of the organization. We knew Phil wanted exactly what we wanted. And we responded. I think our respect for Phil and the general lack of respect for Krause is what helped pull the Chicago Bulls apart. Krause lied about little things my children would lie about. And for what purpose? To show who's boss? We had one of the most successful teams in the history of team sports and this guy is running around playing games with his own troops? I never understood all that and I never will.

The relationship between Phil and Krause had been ruined before the 1997–98 season started. Phil told Jerry, "Stop feeling as though you've made all the right decisions. I'm just as much a reason for this team being successful as you are." That rubbed Krause the wrong way. He might have come from a different era, but I think Krause understood the depth of Phil's impact on the team. He knew why the players liked Phil and he knew why we busted our butts for Phil. But Krause wanted to be the reason we played hard. He wanted to be the guy the players respected and talked to. When Phil signed his last contract, Krause told him, "I don't care if you go 82–0. You're not coming back next season." That's why Phil knew it was over from the beginning of the season.

ALL THAT TALK ABOUT BRINGING HIM BACK FOR ONE MORE YEAR AND KEEPING THE TEAM TOGETHER AFTER OUR SIXTH CHAMPIONSHIP WAS PUBLIC RELATIONS. MANAGEMENT KNEW PHIL WASN'T COMING BACK AND PHIL KNEW MANAGEMENT DIDN'T WANT HIM BACK.

WHAT WOULD YOU DO? HOW COULD YOU RELY ON A GUY LIKE JERRY KRAUSE?

HE WOULDN'T TELL YOU IF THE SUN WAS OUT. BESIDES, PLAYERS NEVER HAD A DAY-TO-DAY RELATIONSHIP WITH HIM. JERRY RESENTED PHIL BECAUSE THE COACH AND PLAYERS HAD A MUTUAL RESPECT.

WE ALL EARNED THAT RESPECT FROM ONE ANOTHER.

WE KNEW PHIL WAS REAL BECAUSE WE COULD SEE HIM EVERY DAY. THERE WAS NO WAY MANAGEMENT COULD HAVE FORCED PHIL TO BE SOME-ONE ELSE. HE HAD A DIFFERENT CONNECTION. HE UNDERSTOOD MANAGEMENT'S VIEWS, BUT PHIL ALSO BELIEVED IN TREATING PLAYERS AS INDIVIDUALS WITHIN THE GROUP. IN A SENSE, THAT WAS HIS GIFT TO US.

PHIL WAS SPECIAL.

EVEN JERRY KRAUSE KNOWS THAT.

F rom the moment training camp started in 1992 I knew we had lost something. The team was no longer connected, and Horace Grant was the first one to break that connection. Horace couldn't accept his level on the team. Scottie and I had gone right from our second championship to the Barcelona Olympics. Our window for getting rest and bouncing back for the 1992–93 season was closing quickly by the time we returned from Spain. Phil understood how we felt and allowed us to practice once a day during the first week of camp. Horace, who had an entire summer off, had to practice twice a day with everyone else and he rebelled. At the same time, some people started whispering in Horace's ear. He was a follower, not a leader, so Horace listened to people tell him how great he was and how

I received freedoms and special attention. My relationship with Horace was never the same. Horace wanted to be at a certain level and Phil wouldn't put him there. So Horace got angry and started creating a wedge within the team. There were things leaked to the media that I said in private or on the team bus. That's when the atmosphere within the team became tense. On the court we did our jobs, but away from the game the harmony Phil had created was disrupted. There were guys I could see whispering to a reporter and the next day there's a quote from an anonymous source. I knew exactly who was saying what and so did everyone else on the team. How can you play with someone when you are afraid of saying something to them in private? Phil knew what was going on, but he had his own problems with B.J. Armstrong. All we needed B.J. to do was step in and fill a role. For a while I was able to deflect a lot of the friction between Phil and B.J. because I could talk to B.J. and I liked him. But he would look at John Paxson and think, "I'm quicker, I can get down the lane faster." What B.J. didn't see was John's savvy. I'm pretty sure if you ask B.J. now he realizes the system was perfect for him, too.

WE ALL HAD TO SUPPRESS OUR

EGOS

FOR THE SYSTEM. THERE WAS A GREATER GOOD, BUT SOME OF THOSE GUYS DIDN'T UNDERSTAND THE CONCEPT.

(J)uanita and I were married before the 1989–90 season in the Little White Chapel in Las Vegas in front of a few friends. There was a reason for me getting married and having children. That experience of being a husband and a father provided a balance and a focus away from basketball. I could have gotten myself in trouble. I don't know what kind of trouble, but if I had

been single, playing basketball, and making a lot of money, I could have made some wrong decisions. That's why I think our lives unfolded the way they did for a reason. When my first son was born, I felt like I became a man in a sense. There was a new level of maturity. Now I was responsible for that child and for the mother of that child. Not tomorrow or the next

During my mother's pregnancy with me, my mother's mother died unexpectedly.
The doctors made my mother stay in bed because they were worried about a miscarriage. According to my father, there was a near miscarriage and there was some question as to whether I would make it or not.
I was born with a nose bleed and my parents were worried that there was something wrong with me.
Later on, when I was a baby, I fell behind my parents' bed and almost suffocated.
Then, when I was about two years old I picked up two wires next to a car my father was working on.
It had been raining and again, according to my father, the shock sent me flying about three feet.
There were a lot of things that happened even as I got older that could have changed everything.
I mean, my girlfriend got swept away in a flood and drowned when we were in college.
Another time, I was swimming with a friend when both of us got pulled into the ocean by a strong undertow. I was able to get free and make it back to land. He never made it back.

HOW CAN YOU SAY THERE ISN'T A PLAN FOR ALL OF US?

day, but every minute of every day. I couldn't think self-ishly anymore. There continue to be sacrifices based on the commitment I have to my family. But it has always been good for me. It provided balance at a time when my life easily could have been out of balance. During that time they didn't know me as anything but Daddy. They didn't know anything about Michael Jordan the superstar basketball player who did all kinds of endorsement deals. I was a father and a husband. They wouldn't have allowed me to be anything else. That was fine with me.

BY 1992 I
WAS BEGINNING
TO FEEL LIKE
A FISH IN
A FISHBOWL.

MY LIFE WAS CHANGING AND THE WAY I WAS PERCEIVED WAS CHANGING, TOO. I WAS A FATHER AND A HUSBAND AT HOME, BUT EVERYWHERE ELSE I WAS MICHAEL JORDAN. AND IT SEEMED LIKE EVERYONE HAD AN IDEA OF WHAT THAT MEANT EXCEPT ME. EARLY IN MY CAREER I REALLY COULDN'T GET A SENSE OF WHO I WAS FROM THE FAN'S PERSPECTIVE. I DIDN'T FEEL AS FAMOUS AS PEOPLE SAID I WAS. I WAS SO FOCUSED ON THE GAME THAT I DIDN'T HAVE TIME TO STEP BACK AND CONSIDER MY LIFE IN THE CONTEXT OF EVERYONE ELSE. TO SOME DEGREE, I THINK THAT'S WHY I WAS SO WELL RECEIVED. I WASN'T ACTING. I WASN'T TRYING TO BE SOMETHING I WASN'T. I ALWAYS FELT COMFORTABLE IN THE SPOTLIGHT BECAUSE I WAS JUST BEING MYSELF.

✦ WITH MY PERSONALITY AND THE WAY I WAS RAISED, IT WOULD HAVE BEEN IMPOSSIBLE TO BE SOMETHING ELSE. MY PARENTS NEVER WOULD HAVE ALLOWED ME TO GET AWAY WITH SOME KIND OF ACT. I NEVER CONSIDERED MYSELF BETTER THAN ANYONE ELSE, NOT EVEN ON THE BASKETBALL COURT. I WANTED TO GET TO THE TOP AND I HAD A PRETTY GOOD IDEA OF WHAT IT TOOK. ✦ BUT LIFE ON A PEDESTAL CAN BE LONELY EVEN WITH A SUPPORTIVE FAM-ILY. WE WERE WINNING, I WAS PLAYING WELL, AND EVERYONE WAS SAFE. BUT I STARTED TO FEEL THE ATTENTION TAKE ON A DIFFERENT TONE. NO ONE WAS CRITICIZING MY BASKETBALL ANYMORE, SO THEY STARTED GOING AFTER ME PERSONALLY. I KNEW THAT TIME WOULD COME. IT ALWAYS DOES. IN A WAY, THAT'S THE BEAUTY OF AMERICA. WE HAVE THE FREEDOM TO BUILD PEOPLE UP AND TEAR THEM DOWN. EVERYONE CAN HAVE THEIR OWN OPINION AND I RESPECT THAT. ✦ BY THE BEGINNING OF THE 1992–93 SEASON, I WAS TIRED, PHYSICALLY AND MENTALLY. I HAD PLAYED FOR ALMOST TWO YEARS STRAIGHT, THERE HAD BEEN ONE MINOR CONTROVERSY AFTER ANOTHER, AND THE COHESIVE UNIT PHIL JACKSON HAD CRE-ATED WAS STARTING TO COME APART. I COULD SEE THE EFFECT SUCCESS WAS HAVING ON CERTAIN PEOPLE. I KNEW THE NEXT 12 MONTHS WOULD BE DIFFICULT. BUT I HAD NO IDEA HOW HARD THEY WOULD BE AND JUST HOW MUCH MY LIFE WOULD CHANGE. ✦

I DIDN'T PRACTICE ZEN OR SIT IN A ROOM AND MEDITATE.

But Phil provided each of us with something we could incorporate into our lives. He didn't force-feed us, he just provided options. He presented the thoughts intelligently. You could say there was some wisdom in his approach. He would appear to direct a thought or idea to the entire team, but usually the message was meant for an individual player. If you were that player, you got the message even though it was delivered to the entire group. That was one of Phil's gifts, his ability to talk to us individually within the collective. It's what tied us all together. I realized early on that some of the practices Phil spoke about I had been doing innately my entire life. For example, Phil brought in a sports psychologist to talk about getting into the zone. Well, I had been there before so I understood the concept. I understood the rhythm of the moment and how the game starts flowing toward you. I just couldn't comprehend how to get myself in the zone consistently. He provided methods and practices designed to get us into the zone all the time. To achieve that level of awareness and understanding real- ly involves a level of perfection. I'm still not sure we are meant to understand how to think in a man- ner that allows a player to spend an entire 48 minutes in the zone. I relied upon game situations to find that rhythm. But all these concepts gave me something to think about, to challenge myself with mentally. Sometimes it was hard to find a challenge physically, especially when I came back from baseball. But I have always been in tune with my body. When we first started meditating during stretching before practice, I thought it was crazy. I'm closing one eye and keeping the other eye open to see what other fool is doing this besides me. Eventually I became more accepting because I could see everyone making an effort. I opened my mind to meditation and Phil's teachings. My mind still travels a little bit, but Phil taught us to concentrate on breathing to bring the mind back to center. There are certain times when I incorporate those thoughts into my daily life, but I certainly haven't mastered the concepts yet. •

I'm sure no one noticed, but Dean Smith 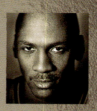 came up to Chicago for a playoff game in 1993. We had talked all season about me leaving the game. Up to that point he never had seen me play an NBA game in person. After a long talk in April, he asked if this was the end and I told him, "Yes, it is." I needed a change because I no longer had the motivation that had carried

AS EARLY AS THE 1992 OLYMPICS

me to that point in my career. I would talk to Coach Smith every other week. I still do. We would talk about life,

I KNEW THE NEXT SEASON

the family, what was happening with the team, how I was feeling mentally and physically. As the season pro-

WOULD BE MY LAST. I HAD TALKED IT OVER

gressed I knew he could sense my desire to leave. He never once tried to talk me out of it. He just wanted to

WITH MY FATHER AND HE KNEW I WAS

understand where I was mentally and how I had come to that decision. He said, "It has been a great run, you've

MENTALLY DRAINED. I NEEDED A BREAK AND

accomplished a lot, and you have had a lot of pressure. You probably do need a break." He always took that

I CONSIDERED LEAVING AFTER OUR

approach. He never tried to change a person's mind. Even when I was coming out of school, Dean never tried

SECOND CHAMPIONSHIP. THE ONLY REASON

to talk me into staying despite the fact my leaving was going to have an impact on his program. He knew I was

I CAME BACK WAS TO WIN

getting mentally exhausted. We had won back-to-back titles, my time between seasons had been eliminated by

A THIRD STRAIGHT CHAMPIONSHIP,

the Olympics, and people were starting to pick away at me personally. There were also a lot of things happening

WHICH WAS SOMETHING NEITHER

with the team that told me it was time to make a change. Everyone enjoyed being on top of the hill but they

LARRY NOR MAGIC HAD DONE.

were starting to take shortcuts. It became such an unbelievable burden to constantly answer the critics, questions

about Horace's contract, and all the sniping that was taking place between players. I didn't want any long good-

byes and I certainly didn't want a season-long ceremony. By the time the 1993 playoffs started I had made up

my mind. It was the perfect time. I knew it, my father knew it, and Dean knew it. No one else had a clue.

IF YOU PRACTICE THE WAY YOU PLAY, THERE SHOULDN'T BE ANY DIFFERENCE. THAT'S WHY I PRACTICED SO HARD.

I WANTED TO BE PREPARED FOR THE GAME.

I PRACTICED HARD ENOUGH THAT THE GAMES WERE OFTEN EASIER. THAT'S EXACTLY WHAT I WAS TRYING TO ACHIEVE. NO ONE CAN TURN IT ON WITHOUT PREPARING THEMSELVES IN PRACTICE. I HAD TO PRACTICE AS HARD AS I COULD SO ANYTHING WAS POSSIBLE ONCE THE GAME STARTED. I LOVED THE COMPETITION OF PRACTICE. I GOT THAT FROM NORTH CAROLINA, WHERE COACH SMITH WOULD MAKE EVERY DRILL COMPETITIVE. THAT GROWS ON YOU, SO EVERYTHING WE DID IN PRACTICE BECAME COMPETITIVE. I TOOK PRIDE IN THE WAY I PRACTICED.

The fourth quarter of a basketball game changes the dynamics of the game for players. My focus would become clearer while other players lost their focus as the pressure mounted. A lot of times I was able to dominate in he fourth quarter because as I channeled myself into the game, my opponent was doing just the opposite, which doubled the impact of my attack. As the momentum starts to turn, the first thought for most players is a negative one. I never went into the fourth quarter of a game thinking we couldn't win. If I ever let a negative thought slip in, then I might as well have sat down. As long as I felt we could win, then believe me, brother, we are going to have an opportunity to win. Going into Game 6 of the 1998 Finals against Utah we went into the fourth quarter down three points. That was nothing. And it was nothing even with one of our key players out. My whole thought process was always, "We're going to win this game. I don't know how, but I believe we are going to win." It didn't matter whether we were down 4 points or 24 points. I always felt things would work out. During the 1997–98 season I built toward the fourth quarter because I was conserving energy early in the game. My game had always been to go all out for 48 minutes. Now I was conserving myself for the last 12 minutes.

third

PLAYING PHOENIX
AND CHARLES BARKLEY IN THE 1993 FINALS
WAS LIKE PLAYING AGAINST YOUR LITTLE BROTHER
AND KNOWING YOU'RE WELL-EQUIPPED.

YOUR LITTLE BROTHER MIGHT BEAT YOU
ONE OR TWO OUT OF SEVEN, BUT YOU KNOW
HE'S GOING TO GET BEAT IN THE END.

THE SUNS DIDN'T KNOW HOW TO WIN.
THEY KNEW HOW TO COMPETE,
BUT THEY DIDN'T KNOW HOW TO WIN.
THERE IS A DIFFERENCE.

1992 NBA FINALS COMPARISON

JORDAN		BARKLEY
6	G	6
274	MIN	277
199	FGA	126
101	FGM	60
49	FTA	56
34	FTM	42
51	RB	78
38	AST	33
10	STL	7
4	BLK	3
246	PTS	164
41.0	AVG	27.3
55	HI	42

MY FATHER'S DEATH ENDED ONE OF THE MOST SUCCESSFUL AND DIFFICULT PERIODS OF MY LIFE.

HE WAS MY BEST FRIEND AND HE KNEW EVERYTHING ABOUT ME.

HE KNEW THINGS THAT WERE GOING TO HAPPEN TO ME LONG BEFORE THEY HAPPENED. THE LIGHT SIDE OF MY PERSONALITY COMES FROM MY

FATHER. HE WAS A PEOPLE PERSON AND HE HAD A GREAT SENSE OF HUMOR. HE TAUGHT ME A LOT ABOUT LIFE,

AND ONE OF THOSE LESSONS WAS THAT EVERYTHING HAPPENS FOR A REASON.

That's why I was able to remain positive about life, my life, after my father's death. I look at that experience as God's way of telling me it was time to stand up and make decisions by myself. I no longer had the support and guidance of my father to fall back on. It was my time to become more mature in my approach to life. Everything I had done to that point, from basketball to business, I passed by my parents. I valued their opinion and to some extent I felt I needed their guidance. When he died I realized I had to start making those decisions independent of everyone else. I could still ask for advice and I would listen, but the responsibility was mine alone. I had to make the kind of decisions men make and I had to make them for myself without that shoulder to lean on. That doesn't mean he's not here with me at every moment. I can feel him. I know he's with me. I have all the life lessons and teachings he provided me in the 30 years I was around him. And I have his voice, his presence.

I know he's watching. I know how he's reacting to my success, the way my children are growing and how my life with Juanita has grown. So I look back at that period and his death as a test. But I also know I'll be taking that test for the rest of my life.

A COUPLE WEEKS AFTER OUR THIRD CHAMPIONSHIP I KNEW I WAS THROUGH. JERRY REINSDORF AND DAVID FALK TALKED ME INTO TAKING THE SUMMER TO THINK ABOUT WHAT I WANTED TO DO. BUT I KNEW. MY FATHER'S DEATH AND EVERYTHING THAT FOLLOWED, THE ATTACKS ON ME AND MY FAMILY, THE SUGGESTION THAT I WAS SOMEHOW TO BLAME OR THAT MY GAMBLING PLAYED A ROLE, ONLY HELPED TO CONFIRM WHAT I KNEW MONTHS BEFORE. I NEEDED A BREAK. IN EARLY SEPTEMBER I MET WITH PHIL IN HIS OFFICE AT THE BERTO CENTER. I HAD BEEN IN THERE MANY TIMES BEFORE AND I KNEW I WOULDN'T BE IN THERE TOO MANY MORE TIMES IN THE FUTURE. I DIDN'T TAKE A LOT OF TIME.

I JUST ASKED HIM TO GIVE ME A REASON TO KEEP PLAYING.

Phil looked at me for a second or two and then talked about how I had a God-given gift and that I had a responsibility to use that gift for the benefit of others. I said I understood and that I agreed with his reasoning. But at some point in time I was going to retire anyway. What difference did it make if that time was now or two years from now? My gift would be taken away sooner or later, whether I liked it or not. Age and the simple passage of time would see to that. Phil looked at me and tried to make another point or two, but at that moment I knew what I was going to do. He just couldn't come up with a good enough reason for me to continue playing. And I didn't have one, either.

MICHAEL JORDAN

CHICAGO BULLS
1984 — 1993

The best there ever was. The best there ever will be.

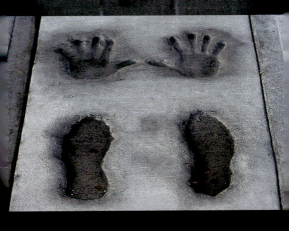

IT WAS LIKE BEING A KID AGAIN.

My father and I talked about baseball all the time because of what Bo Jackson and Deion Sanders were doing. He always had an idea about me playing baseball because he had started me in the game when I was growing up. I started getting invitations to play a game or two for minor league teams in the early 1990s. Muggsy Bogues and Del Curry had played a little bit with a team in North Carolina, so my father said, "Why don't you give it a try?" But I never had enough time in the offseason, and besides, I hadn't accomplished everything I wanted to accomplish in basketball. But I knew I'd give it a shot at some point. No one even knew we were having these conversations much less that I was serious about stepping away from the game of basketball. By the summer of 1992 I was ready to commit the entire summer to baseball. The Dream Team and the 1992 Barcelona

I WAS THINKING ABOUT LEAVING BASKETBALL FOR BASEBALL AS FAR BACK AS 1991.

Olympics put my baseball plans on hold. Still, I didn't know for sure I was going to play baseball when I retired. I didn't know whether I'd have the opportunity to play. I went to Jerry Reinsdorf and told him it was something I wanted to pursue. He knew of my interest in the game, so he wasn't caught completely off guard. Neither one of us wanted to make a spectacle of my desire to play, so I started working out privately with Bill Melton, a well-known former White Sox player, and the team's trainer, Herm Schneider. After about eight weeks the news started to leak out and I told the world. I always considered myself a great all-around athlete and I believed I could do anything if I set my mind to it. I was serious about making the White Sox team.

I WAS SWINGING A 34-OUNCE BAT 300 TO 400 TIMES A DAY. I HAD BLISTERS ALL ACROSS MY HANDS EVEN WITH BATTING GLOVES.
HRNIAK, THE WHITE SOX HITTING COACH. I'D HIT WITH WALT FOR AN HOUR OR TWO, THEN GO THROUGH THE ENTIRE

IF ANYONE DIDN'T THINK I WAS SERIOUS
THE BLOOD DRIPPING OFF MY HANDS

BASEBALL. I HAD TO BUILD MYSELF UP FROM MY FINGERTIPS TO MY SHOULDERS.

WHEN WE GOT DOWN TO FLORIDA AND SPRING TRAINING, I WOULD BE THERE AT 6 O'CLOCK EVERY MORNING TO WORK WITH WALT
PRACTICE AND FINISH THE DAY BACK WITH WALT. THAT WAS MY ROUTINE EVERY DAY OF SPRING TRAINING IN 1994.

IT WAS BECAUSE THEY COULD NOT SEE
OR THOSE 6 A.M. BATTING SESSIONS.

LOOK FOR A SLIDER, A CURVEBALL AND FASTBALL, TWO-SEAMERS AND FOUR-SEAMERS, GETTING LEADS, READING A PITCHER FROM FIRST BASE, SLIDING.
HAT WOULD HAPPEN. NOT JERRY REINSDORF, NOT WHITE SOX GENERAL MANAGER RON SCHUELER, NO ONE KNEW WHETHER I WOULD SUCCEED.

HOW WOULD I DESCRIBE MY BASEBALL EXPERIENCE?

I WOULD DESCRIBE IT NOW THE SAME WAY I DESCRIBED IT THEN. EVERY MOMENT WAS A WARM ONE. I REMEMBER LOOKING UP IN THE SKY FROM TIME TO TIME AND BEING AMAZED AT HOW MUCH MY LIFE HAD CHANGED. I HAD NO FEAR. JUST A WARM FEELING. I CAN'T DESCRIBE THE SENSE EXACTLY, BUT NOW IT SEEMS LIKE I WAS LIVING A DREAM. MAYBE IT WAS THE PRESENCE OF MY FATHER THAT MADE THOSE MOMENTS SO WARM. I THOUGHT ABOUT HIM ALL THE TIME. AND I KNEW HE WAS THERE. IT WAS ALMOST LIKE WE WERE TOTALLY CONNECTED DURING THAT TIME.

The White Sox sent me to the Double A team in Birmingham in the Southern League. It turned out to be one of the best times of my life. I was learning, experiencing the game, and at the same time I was teaching the younger guys how to handle certain situations. They wanted to know everything about me and I wanted to know everything they knew about baseball. We were helping one another out in that way. I made sure we had a nicer bus, the team had to upgrade the living conditions on the road for security reasons, and when we went out to eat most of the time it was my treat. I was just happy to be a part of the team. There were a lot of things that felt good. The camaraderie was unbelievable compared to the NBA. We did things in groups, little things like going to dinner. Everything was purer, more genuine. Even the relationships had a purity and innocence to them. I wouldn't change anything about that experience.

I REALLY DIDN'T PAY MUCH ATTENTION TO BASKETBALL DURING BASEBALL. I NEVER THOUGHT I WOULD COME BACK, EITHER. I COULD SEE IMPROVEMENT AND I WAS STARTING TO BECOME COMFORTABLE WITH THE GAME. I HIT .202 AT BIRMINGHAM, BUT I HIT .259 THE LAST MONTH AND PLAYED WELL IN THE ARIZONA WINTER LEAGUE. THERE WERE ONLY FIVE OTHER PLAYERS WHO HAD 50 RBI AND 30 STOLEN BASES IN THE SOUTHERN LEAGUE IN 1994, AND BY THE END OF THE SEASON I WAS FINDING MY POWER. BUT WHEN THE BASEBALL STRIKE STARTED I FELT LIKE I HAD BEEN PUT IN A BOX. I TOLD SCHUELER I DIDN'T WANT TO BE USED TO DRAW FANS INTO SPRING TRAINING GAMES. I DIDN'T WANT ANY PART OF CROSSING A PICKET LINE. THEY PUT ME IN A DIFFICULT SITUATION ANYWAY. I HAD OPTIONS BUT THE YOUNGER GUYS DIDN'T KNOW WHAT TO DO. THEY WERE COMING TO ME FOR ADVICE. SHOULD THEY REFUSE TO PLAY IN THE GAMES AND RISK BEING BLACKBALLED BY MANAGEMENT, OR SHOULD THEY PLAY AND RISK BEING TARGETED BY THE PLAYERS? I FELT SORRY FOR THEM AND I DIDN'T KNOW WHAT TO SAY. WHEN THE WHITE SOX PUT ME IN THE SAME SITUATION I DECIDED TO WALK AWAY INSTEAD OF HELPING THE OWNERS.

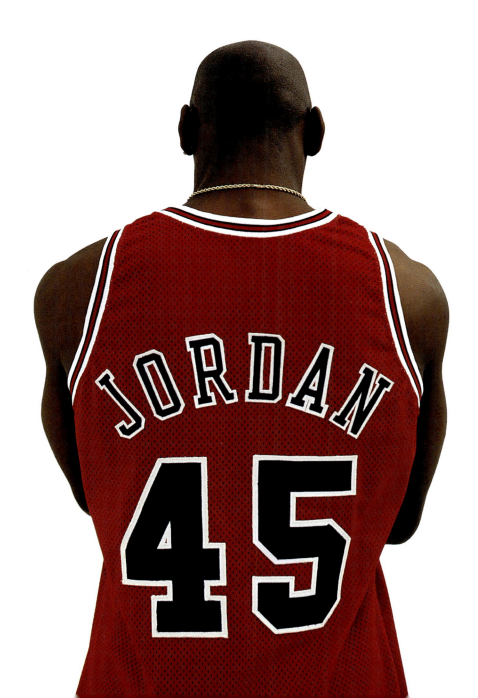

$$45 \div 2 = 22.5$$

WHEN I CAME BACK I DIDN'T WANT TO PLAY WITH THE LAST NUMBER MY FATHER HAD SEEN ME WEAR.

BECAUSE HE WASN'T AROUND,

I THOUGHT OF MY RETURN AS A NEW BEGINNING.

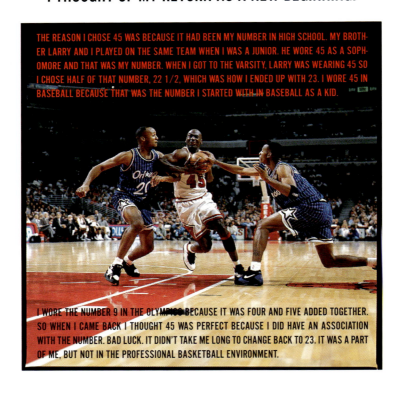

THE REASON I CHOSE 45 WAS BECAUSE IT HAD BEEN MY NUMBER IN HIGH SCHOOL. MY BROTHER LARRY AND I PLAYED ON THE SAME TEAM WHEN I WAS A JUNIOR. HE WORE 45 AS A SOPHOMORE AND THAT WAS MY NUMBER. WHEN I GOT TO THE VARSITY, LARRY WAS WEARING 45 SO I CHOSE HALF OF THAT NUMBER, 22 1/2, WHICH WAS HOW I ENDED UP WITH 23. I WORE 45 IN BASEBALL BECAUSE THAT WAS THE NUMBER I STARTED WITH IN BASEBALL AS A KID.

I WORE THE NUMBER 9 IN THE OLYMPICS BECAUSE IT WAS FOUR AND FIVE ADDED TOGETHER. SO WHEN I CAME BACK I THOUGHT 45 WAS PERFECT BECAUSE I DID HAVE AN ASSOCIATION WITH THE NUMBER. BAD LUCK. IT DIDN'T TAKE ME LONG TO CHANGE BACK TO 23. IT WAS A PART OF ME, BUT NOT IN THE PROFESSIONAL BASKETBALL ENVIRONMENT.

$$\begin{array}{r} 4 \\ +5 \\ \hline 9 \end{array}$$

The first time everything clicked was my third game back against the Knicks in New York. I dropped a double nickel on them. I was still physically prepared to play baseball at that point. That game was strictly off talent. My game up to that point was up and down. You knew physically I wasn't ready to play because I couldn't consistently do my job. The guys hadn't seen me for a while so I think they forgot how I played. They let

John Starks guard me one-on-one and they didn't double team. I was bigger than John and I could turn around and shoot over him all night long. They let me get into that zone. I think the fact the game was in Madison Square Garden had something to do with my performance. I always wanted to play well in New York because it's a basketball mecca.

DOUBLE NICKEL

WE GOT KNOCKED OUT OF THE 1995 PLAYOFFS BY ORLANDO
AND I KNEW I HAD A LOT OF WORK TO DO. I TOLD DAVID FALK

THERE WAS NO WAY I WOULD DO THE MOVIE "SPACE JAM" UNLESS I WAS ABLE TO WORK OUT

AND PLAY ON THE WARNER BROS. LOT.

There was no way I could stay out there for eight weeks after getting knocked out of the playoffs and being criticized for coming back. I said, "David, I need the work. I have got to practice. I need to play." He says, "What if we can create a working environment for you on the set that allows you to still do the movie?" I said, "Show me." So they built this state-of-the-art gymnasium that covered an entire parking lot. It had airconditioning, stereo system, card tables, seats, lights, every conceivable weight-lifting machine, everything I needed. I would go over to the gym at lunch to lift weights and then return from about 7:00 to 9:30 every night to play. There was never a camera in the place. Reggie Miller and Chris Mills were there every single day. Charles Oakley came out and played, Magic came out the last day, Tim Hardaway, Dennis Rodman, all the UCLA players, Tracy Murray was there every day, Lamond Murray, Reggie Theus, Jawann Howard, Larry Johnson, Rod Strickland, Grant Hill, all kinds of guys came into town. The games were great. Oakley took over the middle and played just like he did during the season. Reggie and Eddie Jones went at it pretty good. I knew why these guys showed up. They wanted to learn and to try to get a feel for the way I played. I knew their strategy. But they didn't know I was doing the same. I always felt like I could learn faster than other people. So they were helping me just like I was helping them. I could feel it coming back pretty quickly.

72

I COULDN'T WAIT FOR THE 1995–96 SEASON TO START. I KNEW MY GAME HAD COME BACK WITH ALL THE WORK I PUT IN OVER THE SUMMER. I FELT LIKE A KID COMING OUT OF COLLEGE WITH SOMETHING TO PROVE. THE CONSENSUS WAS THAT I HAD LOST A STEP, BUT THERE WAS NO STOPPING US THAT SEASON. WE GOT OFF TO A GREAT START. WE WON 18 IN A ROW AT ONE POINT AND WERE ROLLING. WE HAD A SWAGGER ABOUT OURSELVES BECAUSE WE WERE DOMINATING. THEY KNEW WHAT WE WERE RUNNING, BUT WE JUST PICKED OPPOSING TEAMS APART. EVERYBODY ON THAT TEAM

10

WAS DEDICATED TO PLAYING THEIR ROLE BECAUSE MOST OF THEM HAD SOMETHING TO PROVE. NOT EVERYONE HAD WON A CHAMPIONSHIP. DENNIS RODMAN HAD WON IN DETROIT, BUT HE HAD TO PROVE HE COULD BE SOMETHING OTHER THAN A DISRUPTIVE INFLUENCE. OUR APPROACH THAT SEASON WAS RIGHT IN TUNE WITH MY ATTITUDE, WHICH WAS TO WIN AND BE DOMINANT IN THE PROCESS. 72 AND 10? IN THIS ERA WITH 29 TEAMS? INCREDIBLE. THAT WAS THE BEST RHYTHM ANY BULLS TEAM I PLAYED FOR HAD FOR AN ENTIRE SEASON.

THERE'S NOTHING EASY ABOUT

I know some players think they could do what I did if they had the kind of freedom I had. But they don't even have a basic understanding of what it takes to be that consistent over the course of an 82-game season. Before the 1997–98 season, Penny Hardaway told me he was going to win the scoring title and average 40 points a game. Shaquille O'Neal was gone and Hardaway figured he would have all the opportunities. He was serious, too. Do you know how hard it is to average 40 points? That's 10 points a quarter, every quarter of every game. And that's just your average. Now, if you don't score at least 10, then you have to score even more later.

You have to do that while the defense is completely focused on stopping you from scoring. That means you have to fight off double teams, get to the line, and knock down at least 80 percent of your free throws. All those things have to happen every single night. Scoring like I do doesn't happen because a situation changes or a player decides to be more aggressive. You have to study the game, find opportunities. The opportunities you find one night might not be there the next. You have to figure out ways to beat virtually every one of your opponents because you can be darn sure that if you're scoring that many points every one of your

SUNDAY
Games
83
Avg. Points
32.6

MONDAY
Games
68
Avg. Points
30.7

TUESDAY
Games
185
Avg. Points
31.2

WEDNESDAY
Games
120
Avg. Points
32.2

LEADING THE NBA IN SCORING.

opponents is going to make a point of shutting you down. You have to be aggressive at all times mentally, then pick and choose when to attack physically. These kids don't understand that. They don't have any understanding of the mental aspect necessary to score 40 points even one night.

You have to be able to adjust constantly. Do you come out at the beginning attacking to distort the entire game to your advantage? Do you try to get everyone else involved so they become a threat and open the floor for you? I haven't even talked about what you have to do at the defensive end to get easy baskets. Steals, blocked shots, break-aways, all those sit-

uations play into a 32-point night. At this stage of their careers, guys such as Hardaway and Grant Hill are getting points strictly off physical talent. Now let's move to the playoffs, where you're playing the same team as many as seven times. The adjustments have to come quicker, sometimes between plays. And you have to do all these things with the objective of winning the game. I don't think any of them are ready for that.

THE CHICAGO BULLS WERE THE PERFECT TEAM FOR DENNIS RODMAN, AND PHIL JACKSON WAS THE PERFECT COACH.
PHIL ALLOWED DENNIS TO DO WHAT HE WANTED, BUT DENNIS KNEW HE HAD TO LOCK IN AND CONNECT

Each of us had the freedom to be individuals and to exhibit our own unique personalities. Phil gave us that. He understood that putting restraints on players also took away some of the avenues players used to relax. Ultimately, that isn't good for the collective. Dennis was probably one of the reasons the wedge between Phil and management went so deep. Management gets nervous when players have the kind of freedom Dennis had. Krause never trusted players enough to provide that kind of space. Management was most comfortable with everyone on an even level with a single set of rules. Phil understood some players deserved more advantages than others. Dennis could go to Atlantic City and gamble all night and then plug in and get 25 rebounds. So he earned the freedom Phil granted him. Where did Phil come up with that philosophy? I have no idea. But I do know it

WITH THE REST OF THE TEAM AT GAME TIME. I DIDN'T CARE IF HE RAN OFF ON HIS SIDE TRIPS, OR STAYED OUT ALL NIGHT DOING WHATEVER IT WAS HE DID. BUT WHEN WE ALL ARRIVED AT THE ARENA WE ALL HAD TO PLUG INTO ONE ANOTHER.

was accepted and respected by every player. If you showed him you could go your own way and still plug back into the team at game time, then he would allow you space. At the same time, if Phil ever felt those freedoms jeopardized our approach, he never had a problem pulling back the reins on anybody, including me, to bring the collective thought process back together. He was a player, he had been on championship teams, he had been in an environment with intelligent teammates who were independent and able to make choices. That's why Dennis found a home with the Bulls. That doesn't mean there weren't some harsh words from time to time. There were, usually from me. But our atmosphere allowed Dennis the freedom to be himself within the context of a professional basketball team trying to win championships. In that respect, the Chicago Bulls were unique.

IT SEEMED LIKE EVERYTHING HAD FALLEN INTO PLACE
FOR GAME 6 OF THE 1996 FINALS AGAINST SEATTLE.
I HAD COME BACK WITHOUT MY FATHER,
EVERYBODY WAS QUESTIONING WHAT I HAD DONE
UP TO THAT POINT AND WHAT MORE GRATIFICATION
COULD I POSSIBLY GET OTHER THAN

WINNING THE CHAMPIONSHIP
ON FATHER'S DAY AS A TRIBUTE TO MY FATHER.

fourth

(1) T COULDN'T HAVE PLAYED OUT ANY BETTER. I WAS SO DETERMINED THAT DAY. IT WAS LIKE SOMETIMES YOU GET SO ANGRY THAT YOU CRY. THAT'S HOW DETERMINED I WAS TO WIN THAT GAME. I WAS SO ANGRY AND SO HAPPY AT THE SAME TIME. THERE WAS NO WAY I COULD CONTROL MY EMOTIONS. I WAS ANGRY BECAUSE I FELT LIKE I HAD TO WIN ANOTHER CHAMPIONSHIP BEFORE ANYONE WOULD GIVE CREDENCE TO MY RETURN. BUT I WAS HAPPY THAT I PROVED MY POINT. I HAD LOVED THE GAME FOR SO LONG AND DONE SO MUCH IN THE GAME AND YET I WAS STILL BEING CRITICIZED. ONCE I GRABBED THAT BALL AND THE GAME WAS OVER IT HIT ME AS TO WHAT HAD JUST TRANSPIRED, I HAD COME ALL THE WAY BACK. THERE HAD BEEN SOME DISAPPOINTMENTS ALONG THE WAY, BUT THEY TAUGHT ME TO DO THE RIGHT THING. IF YOU DO THE WORK, YOU GET REWARDED. THERE ARE NO SHORTCUTS IN LIFE.

(J)eff Malone was one of the toughest guys I played against during my career. I could play solid defense against him and he still could make big baskets. Mitch Richmond was definitely difficult for me. But Malone had a unique style. He had a great fallaway jump shot. I could play solid defense and he still could get that shot off. Mitch plays well without the ball, he's savvy at the offensive end and he's strong. We had similar styles in that sense. From day one I liked Mitch. Just like from day one I liked Ray Allen because he has a lot of skills. Early in my career guys like World B Free and George Gervin gave me problems. I was young and I had never seen such smooth play. I had some good battles with Otis Birdsong and Micheal Ray Richardson. Alvin

Robertson was tough. He always gambled on defense too much, though. He was a hands-on, scrappy-type player. Physically he'd bang you. Joe Dumars was tough but he always got help. He was very, very smart. Reggie Miller is tough because he knows how to get you into foul trouble and he's not afraid to take a shot from any distance. Defensively, I didn't have a problem with Reggie. When I wanted to take advantage of Reggie physically I could do that offensively. He presented some problems, but once I got a feel for him I knew how to force him to his weakness.

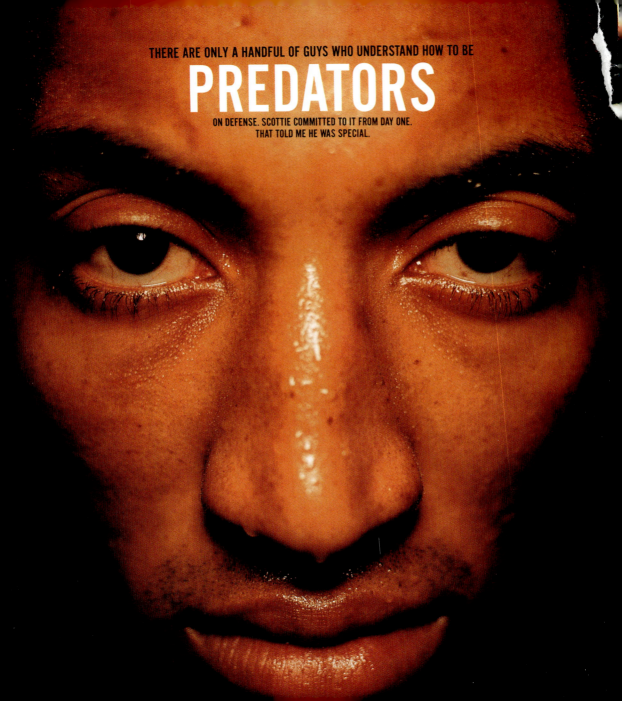

THERE ARE ONLY A HANDFUL OF GUYS WHO UNDERSTAND HOW TO BE

PREDATORS

ON DEFENSE. SCOTTIE COMMITTED TO IT FROM DAY ONE.
THAT TOLD ME HE WAS SPECIAL.

VERY FEW GUYS COME INTO THE NBA WITH THE IDEA OF DOING ALL THE THANKLESS TASKS NECESSARY FOR A TEAM TO WIN. THEY USUALLY ARE FOCUSED ON SCORING POINTS AND PLAYING ENOUGH MINUTES TO PAD THEIR STATS.

From my perspective there are very, very few players I came across in my career who I would consider to have achieved greatness. I would say Magic Johnson and Larry Bird achieved greatness to a certain extent. I was able to learn from their example and take it a step further by becoming a factor at both ends of the court. The only other player I think is close to them is Scottie Pippen. He's an intelligent player, and he understands the game. He had to learn how to be a warrior, how to be aggressive at all times, but Scottie did that. It's not what he can do offensively, but it's what Scottie Pippen can do defensively that puts him in that class. He's right there with those guys in every facet of the game except as a leader. Scottie has leadership qualities, but I didn't know if he wanted that role. In his defense, Scottie came from a smaller environment. It's like a kid growing up in the country playing against kids who grew up in the city. The kid in the country can learn how to play the city game, but it might take him a little longer. In that sense, Bird and Magic came into the league ready to teach. Scottie came into the league ready to learn. Believe me, I think he's a lot closer to those guys than people think. There were a lot of times when I felt like I was playing with my twin. That's how much he grew in the time we played together. I still think I could break him down offensively and I have mastered some of the nuances of the game to a greater degree. It was always a good match. But there is one difference: Scottie learned how to be a predator which meant attacking all the time but still being able to surprise the opponent. The difference between us was that Scottie was an attacker as long as he knew he had a pack of wolves with him. I was an attacker without a pack of wolves. That's a big difference.

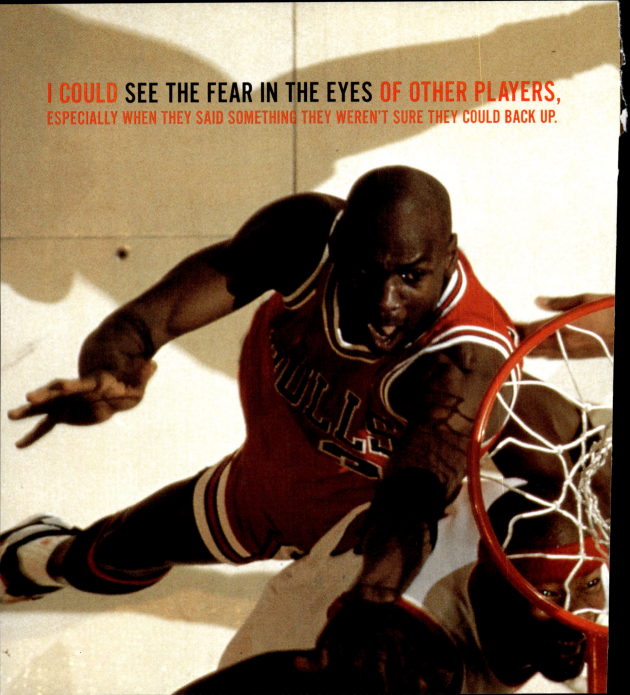

I COULD SEE THE FEAR IN THE EYES OF OTHER PLAYERS, ESPECIALLY WHEN THEY SAID SOMETHING THEY WEREN'T SURE THEY COULD BACK UP.

Let's say someone swears he's going to play better the next night. But once the game starts that player misses his first shot. At that moment you can detect the slightest hesitation, the first hint of fear. Instead of looking at the situation and saying, "OK, I have a good feel for the game now. I'll make the next one," one negative starts building upon another. It's like they start building this wall, one negative piled upon another, until they have no chance of finding a way to knock it down. If I missed a shot, so what? I had the freedom to accept the consequence. I wasn't going to let a missed shot or a mistake affect the rest of my night. I never allowed the negatives to carry over and pile up. In those moments I relied upon past experience. I'd go back to games where I missed my first five shots and then made the next ten. I would try to bring that confidence into the moment. Why would I worry about a shot I hadn't even taken yet? That kind of thinking limits everyone, not just athletes. They aren't comfortable with their skills and they don't have a good connection with their inner being. I tried to improve each and every day. I needed to be able to look back to yesterday and feel like I'm better today. During the game it was a matter of keeping your poise, learning how to settle your nerves in the heat of the moment. I would look for easy opportunities to settle my mind, so I could let the game come to me instead of chasing it all night. That's one of the differences between a good player and a great one.

WHEN I WAS A KID I ALWAYS LIKED TO DRESS UP ON SUNDAYS.
MY BROTHERS AND SISTERS WANTED TO WEAR JEANS, BUT I WORE A COAT AND TIE.
FROM MY PERSPECTIVE, I VIEWED WEARING A COAT AND TIE AS BEING DRESSED UP.

I REMEMBER MY FATHER TELLING ME HOW IMPORTANT FIRST IMPRESSIONS CAN BE FOR SOME PEOPLE. AT NORTH CAROLINA WE WORE SUITS EVERY TIME WE TRAVELED, AND THAT WAS RIGHT UP MY ALLEY. WE WERE TRAVELING TOGETHER AND WE WANTED TO LOOK PRESENTABLE, DIGNIFIED. THAT'S WHY I TOOK THE TIME TO GET COMPLETELY DRESSED IN MY ROOM BEFORE LEAVING FOR THE ARENA. I WANTED TO PRESENT MYSELF IN A WAY THAT WOULD GIVE PEOPLE THE PROPER IMPRESSION OF ME. I WANTED THEM TO KNOW I CARED ABOUT WHAT THEY THOUGHT. IN A SMALL WAY, I WAS ABLE TO SHOW MY RESPECT FOR THEM, TOO.

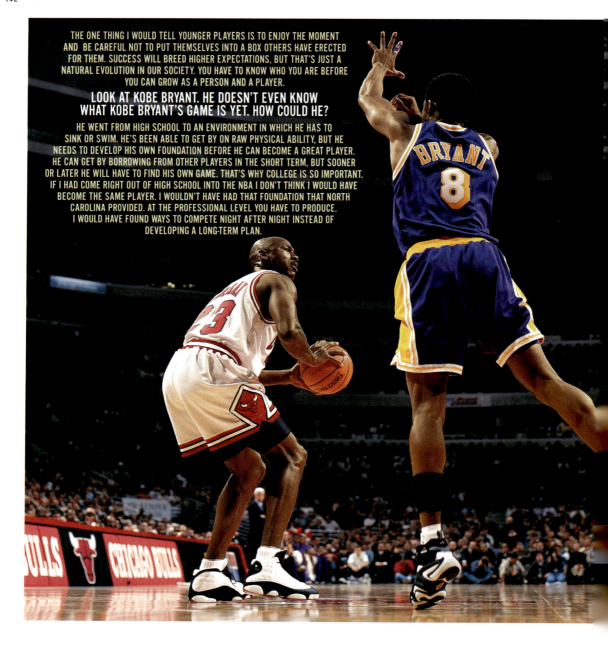

THE ONE THING I WOULD TELL YOUNGER PLAYERS IS TO ENJOY THE MOMENT
AND BE CAREFUL NOT TO PUT THEMSELVES INTO A BOX OTHERS HAVE ERECTED
FOR THEM. SUCCESS WILL BREED HIGHER EXPECTATIONS, BUT THAT'S JUST A
NATURAL EVOLUTION IN OUR SOCIETY. YOU HAVE TO KNOW WHO YOU ARE BEFORE
YOU CAN GROW AS A PERSON AND A PLAYER.

LOOK AT KOBE BRYANT. HE DOESN'T EVEN KNOW
WHAT KOBE BRYANT'S GAME IS YET. HOW COULD HE?

HE WENT FROM HIGH SCHOOL TO AN ENVIRONMENT IN WHICH HE HAS TO
SINK OR SWIM. HE'S BEEN ABLE TO GET BY ON RAW PHYSICAL ABILITY, BUT HE
NEEDS TO DEVELOP HIS OWN FOUNDATION BEFORE HE CAN BECOME A GREAT PLAYER.
HE CAN GET BY BORROWING FROM OTHER PLAYERS IN THE SHORT TERM, BUT SOONER
OR LATER HE WILL HAVE TO FIND HIS OWN GAME. THAT'S WHY COLLEGE IS SO IMPORTANT.
IF I HAD COME RIGHT OUT OF HIGH SCHOOL INTO THE NBA I DON'T THINK I WOULD HAVE
BECOME THE SAME PLAYER. I WOULDN'T HAVE HAD THAT FOUNDATION THAT NORTH
CAROLINA PROVIDED. AT THE PROFESSIONAL LEVEL YOU HAVE TO PRODUCE.
I WOULD HAVE FOUND WAYS TO COMPETE NIGHT AFTER NIGHT INSTEAD OF
DEVELOPING A LONG-TERM PLAN.

CAN KOBE BRYANT BECOME
A GREAT PLAYER?

SURE. BUT IT'S GOING TAKE A LOT MORE EFFORT TO REFINE HIS SKILLS
AT THE SAME TIME HE'S TRYING TO SURVIVE.

Young players also need to know what makes them happy off the floor. What brightens your day? I don't think a lot of players ever gain that knowledge about themselves. They think they know. They think watching videos, going out to clubs, or hanging out with a different woman every night is the answer. If that's what you think makes you truly happy, then you're going to get burned, because it's fleeting. What are you left with when that's been your focus night after night? Those are the kinds of things I try to tell young players. Those are the kinds of conversations I have with Tiger Woods, too. Slow down. Enjoy life. Take it easy. Don't make it difficult. I think with all that was thrown at Tiger so quickly, he felt, quite naturally, that he had to live up to the hype. No one can live up to that kind of hype. I learned that a long time ago. It's something Tiger will have to learn if he wants to perform at a high level and maintain that level for a long time. When I was 21 I was still eating McDonald's food every day. I wasn't trying to search for the perfect meal, for the perfect attitude, or the perfect technique. It just happened. That was the beauty of it all. These guys need to learn to live for the moment. Let it flow and see what happens. There is only so much you can control anyway. If you don't enjoy the process of becoming successful, then there is no beauty in the achievement. Enjoy the day. There will be another one tomorrow. Enjoy life for the sake of life.

IF I KNEW THEN WHAT I KNOW NOW

about what I would have to go through in Game 5 of the 1997 Finals at Utah,

I DON'T KNOW IF I WOULD PLAY.

If the outcome was guaranteed to be the same, then I'd probably go through it again.
But if the outcome wasn't assured, there's no way I would do it again.

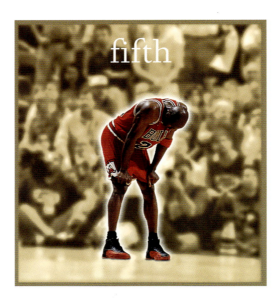

fifth

I COULD HAVE DIED FOR A BASKETBALL GAME.

I PLAYED THAT GAME ON HEART AND DETERMINATION AND NOTHING ELSE.

I didn't have any food, any energy, any sleep, or anything else. I don't even remember a lot about that game.

I have never felt as awful physically as I did in that game.

I woke up at three in the morning with what seemed like stomach flu. I couldn't keep anything down and I couldn't sleep. I took something that I thought would make me drowsy, but the symptoms were so severe I never got back to sleep. By the time I got to the arena I was fighting to stay awake. I just sat back in the locker room drinking coffee, trying to wake up enough to play the game. I didn't have anything in my stomach and the coffee really didn't do anything to wake me up. By halftime I was getting dehydrated, so I started drinking what I thought was Gatorade. But someone had mistakenly handed me a bottle of GatorLode, which is what you

are supposed to drink after you have finished a difficult activity. By the time we went back out for the second half I felt bloated on top of being exhausted. I had continued to drink coffee, which ultimately only helped the dehydration come more quickly. There were times in the third and fourth quarters that I felt like I was going to pass out. I remember thinking, "Get this game over so I can lie down." In the fourth quarter, right before the three-pointer that won the game, I had become almost completely dehydrated. I was shivering, but I continued to sweat. On that last shot, I didn't even know whether it went in or not. I could barely stand up. When I got back into the locker room the doctors were really concerned because I didn't have anything left. I was cold, yet I was sweating and dehydrated. They wanted to give me intravenous fluids, but I made it over to a table, lay down, and starting drinking Gatorade. That's all I did for about 45 minutes. All for a basketball game.

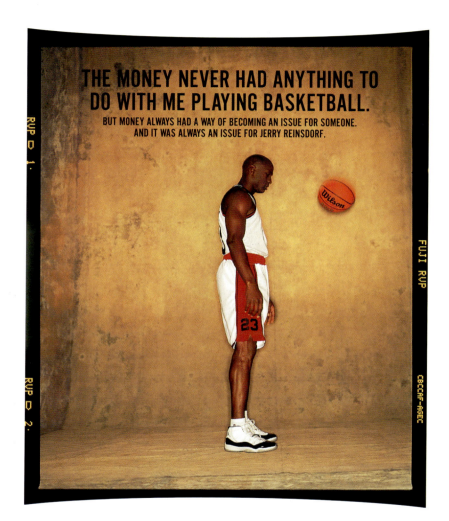

THE MONEY NEVER HAD ANYTHING TO
DO WITH ME PLAYING BASKETBALL.
BUT MONEY ALWAYS HAD A WAY OF BECOMING AN ISSUE FOR SOMEONE.
AND IT WAS ALWAYS AN ISSUE FOR JERRY REINSDORF.

(T)he Bulls knew I wouldn't come back and play for anyone but Phil. After the 1997 championship, they knew they had to sign Phil before they went after me. But they put a clause in Phil's contract that said if I didn't sign by a certain date Phil's deal was void. When we started negotiating my contract for the 1997–98 season everyone knew what I had made the year before. David Falk told the Bulls I deserved a 20 percent raise, the maximum allowed. His feeling was that I had done everything I was paid to do. We won another championship, I won another scoring title, I made the All-Defensive First Team. Jerry's opinion was that I had been paid a lot of money for that performance and I shouldn't get anything more. The discussion eventually went all the way back to my first two contracts and how I wasn't paid market value at the time, so these kinds of numbers were in order to balance the sheets. Finally, I said, "Look, Jerry. My agent is here. You are here. Why don't we split it down the middle, shake hands and get out of here. I'm not out here trying to rob you. I want you to know I lived up to my end of the bargain. I did my job and all I'm asking for is a raise. That could be a dollar or that could be $6 million. I just want an acknowledgment from you that I did my job." All I wanted was the team intact so we could defend our title. I figured both of us had saved face. I was able to have been rewarded for my performance and Jerry was able to say, "OK, we paid you a lot of money, but we also have rewarded you with a number we feel comfortable with." My first thought was, "Great. Now let's go out and do it again." But I knew it never should have come to that kind of discussion. We should have been way past that point, particularly after what happened the year before. Following the 1996 season I signed a one-year deal. Before I left the room, Jerry said something I'll never forget. It changed my opinion of Jerry Reinsdorf. We shook hands and he said, "At some point in time, I know I'm going to regret what we just did." After all these years, after all these championships, after all I had tried to do for the Bulls organization, after all those years of being underpaid and you regret paying me market value? It was like a punch in the heart.

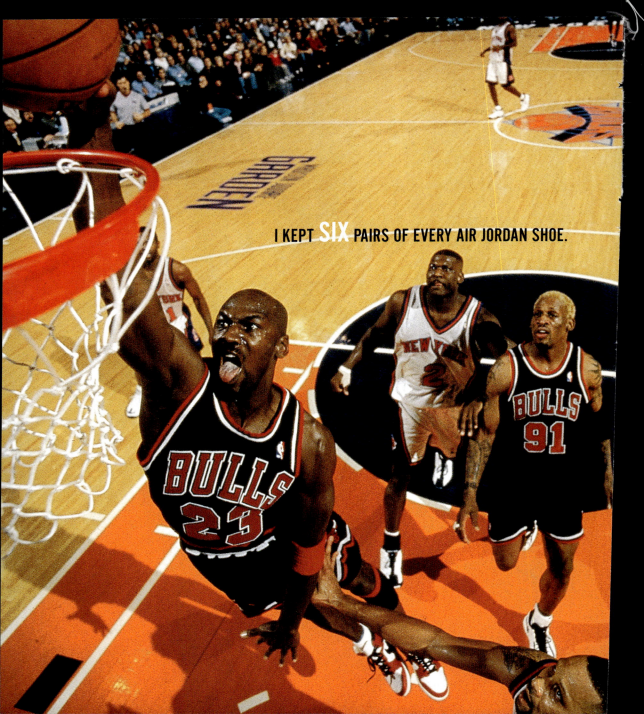

I KEPT **SIX** PAIRS OF EVERY AIR JORDAN SHOE.

MADISON SQUARE GARDEN					FIRST AND LAST GAME BOX SCORE				
FIRST GAME—November 8, 1984: Bulls 121-Knicks 106									
Chicago Bulls starting lineup: Steve Johnson(F), O-lando Woolridge(F), Caldwell Jones(C), Ennis Whatley(G).									
M	FGM	FGA	FTM	FTA	RB	AST	STL	BLK	PTS
33	15	22	3	4	8	5	3	2	33
LAST GAME—March 8, 1998: Bulls 102-Knicks 89									
Chicago Bulls starting lineup: Scottie Pippen(F), Toni Kukoc(F), Dennis Rodman(C), Ron Harper(G).									
M	FGM	FGA	FTM	FTA	RB	AST	STL	BLK	PTS
43	17	33	7	9	8	6	3	1	42

THE NIGHT BEFORE WE WERE LEAVING TO PLAY OUR LAST GAME IN NEW YORK IN 1998, MY WIFE WAS DOING SOME SPRING CLEANING AND MOVED THE SHOES FROM ONE STORAGE CLOSET TO ANOTHER. I THOUGHT,

"THIS MIGHT BE MY LAST TIME IN NEW YORK. LET'S GO BACK TO THE BEGINNING AND WEAR THESE SHOES."

I had worn them before in practice and I thought they were too tight. But it was New York—why not try something different? No one knew I had the shoes in my bag until I started lacing them up. I didn't know for sure I'd wear them in the game until after I tried them out in warm-ups. By then the shoes had caught people's attention, so why not go with it? That's how I approached the game. I wanted to go out there and have a good time. It was a heck of a statement about my feelings for New York. I appreciated playing in New York from the beginning to the end. Plus, we won the game. Their tribute to me was the standing ovation they gave me when I left the court.

sixth

(E)verything leading up to the shot against Utah in Game 6 of the 1998 Finals was vivid. It was like I was watching everything unfold in slow motion on television. I stole the ball, looked up at the clock, and then down the court. I could see every player and I remember exactly where they were as I came up the floor. Steve Kerr was in the corner, John Stockton faked at me and was going to come to me. I was up top. Dennis was curling underneath the post on the left. Scottie was on the bottom post on the right. I could hear sounds, but it was like white noise. In that moment I couldn't distinguish one sound from another, but I was able to evaluate every opportunity on the court. I was going to the right because I knew I could get a shot off. Any time I needed to make a shot I went to my right as long as the defense didn't make a mistake and open a lane to my left. When you go to your right the defensive player

has to come across your body to get to the ball. In Game 1 of the 1997 NBA Finals against Utah, I went left when I hit the game-winning shot because Byron Russell lunged to his left, causing him to be off balance. In 1998, I set myself up to go right again, starting on the left side of the floor. The one thing I didn't want to do was cross over because that would put the ball back into play. All this I knew, but as the shot unfolded, I went through those options instinctively. It unfolded slowly enough for me to evaluate every single thing that was happening. I was able to evalu-

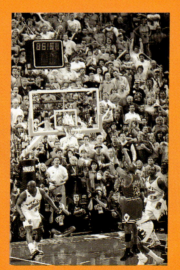

ate the mistake Russell made again and capitalize differently. When he lunged this time I knew exactly what to do. I was going toward Steve Kerr. John Stockton wasn't about to leave Steve open as he had when Steve hit the winning shot in Game 6 of the 1997 Finals. So Stockton faked toward me and went back to Kerr. I had no intention of passing the ball under any circumstances. I figured I stole the ball and it was my opportunity to win or lose the game. I would have taken that shot with five people on me. Ironically, I have problems going to my right for a stop, pull-up jumper because I have a tendency to come up short. I normally fade a little. But on this shot I didn't want to fade because all my jump shots had been short. Think about that. I had enough time to think about those issues. It's incredible, even to me. And yet, that's how it happened. I went straight up and I came straight down.

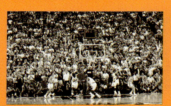

I consciously extended my hand up and out toward the target because I had been coming up short. It looked like I was posing, but it was a fundamentally sound shot. It's truly amazing that I can break down a game into all those parts in that amount of time and then execute the play.

ALL THAT HAPPENED IN ABOUT 11 SECONDS.

WHEN THE NEWS BROKE
DURING THE SUMMER ABOUT
THE BULLS HIRING TIM FLOYD
I WAS DOING MY
BASKETBALL CAMP AT
ELMHURST COLLEGE OUTSIDE CHICAGO.
WE WOULD HAVE
A QUESTION-AND-ANSWER
PERIOD WITH THE KIDS.
USUALLY THEY WOULD ASK
WHAT KIND OF GUM I CHEWED,
STUFF LIKE THAT.
ONE OF THEM ASKED ME WHY
I DIDN'T WANT TO PLAY
FOR A COACH OTHER THAN
PHIL JACKSON.
I SAID, "LET ME GIVE YOU
A COMPARISON. IF YOU GREW
UP YOUR ENTIRE LIFE
WITH ONE SET OF PARENTS AND
YOU GOT TO A CERTAIN AGE AND
YOU WERE ASSIGNED NEW PARENTS,
WHAT WOULD YOU WANT?
WOULD YOU WANT TO STAY WITH
YOUR ORIGINAL PARENTS OR
WITH THE NEW PARENTS?
THE OLD PARENTS WERE THE PEOPLE
WHO TAUGHT YOU EVERYTHING,
FED YOU, HELPED YOU THROUGH
CERTAIN PERIODS OF YOUR LIFE.
NOW THEY SAY YOU HAVE TO GO
THROUGH THE SAME PROCESS
WITH NEW PARENTS?"
THAT'S HOW I FEEL ABOUT PLAYING
FOR ANOTHER COACH.

ALTHOUGH IT WOULD HAVE BEEN HARD TO PLAY FOR ANOTHER COACH,
I ALWAYS WONDERED HOW IT WOULD HAVE BEEN TO PLAY FOR NEW YORK.
GIVEN THE FACTS OF PHIL'S DEPARTURE AND THE BULLS' DESIRE TO REBUILD, I WOULD HAVE SERIOUSLY CONSIDERED PLAYING
FOR THE KNICKS DURING THE 1998-99 SEASON IF I WERE SINGLE.
NEW YORK FANS APPRECIATE GOOD PLAYERS AND I ALWAYS ENJOYED PLAYING IN MADISON SQUARE GARDEN.

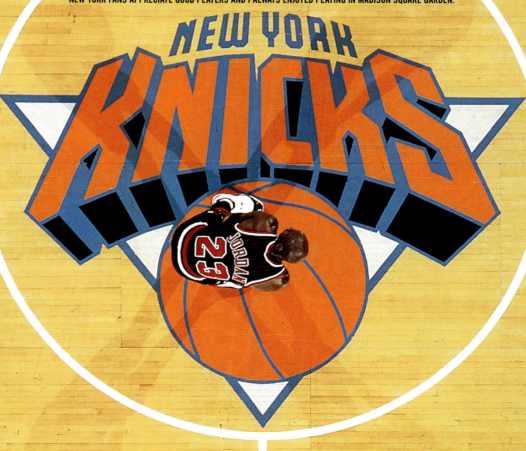

**TOMORROW I DON'T KNOW
WHAT I'M GOING TO DO.
I THINK ABOUT TODAY.
PEOPLE DON'T BELIEVE
I DON'T KNOW WHAT'S
GOING TO HAPPEN NEXT WEEK,
NEXT MONTH, OR NEXT YEAR.**

BUT I TRULY LIVE IN THE MOMENT.

That's what retirement means. You can design and choose your moment. I can design shoes one day and ski the next. I have created the opportunity to have a choice. That is how I am going to live. I am not going to determine what the moment is going to be a week from now. I've never done that and I don't like living that way. I would feel too confined. To me, retirement is having no restraints. I won't be retired fully until I don't have to do anything. One day I won't have to do commercials, or talk to a board, or help in the design of shoes. I will be able to wake up when I wake up. As long as I live in the moment I don't believe I will ever get bored. I am not going to mind being out of the spotlight.

MY PROBLEM IS THAT EVERYONE EXPECTS ME TO LIVE IN THE FUTURE.

Where did it come from? I don't know. That's like asking an artist where his inspiration comes from. Phil Jackson told us many times to deal with what's happening right now. It's an idea that always has been with me. My heart and my soul are in the moment. The best thing about living that way is that you don't know what the next moment is going to bring. And that was the best thing about the way I played the game. No one, not even me, knew what I was going to do next. If I had to pick one characteristic about my game that would be it. I always thought I performed my best when I didn't know what was coming. I didn't know I was going to go out there and score 63 points against the Boston Celtics in my second season. They didn't either and that's why it was a beautiful experience. No one could have expected that to happen. They were stunned, just like I was. What's more beautiful than that?

There is no such thing as a perfect basketball player, and I don't believe there is only one greatest player either. Everyone plays in different eras. I built my talents on the shoulders of someone else's talent. I believe greatness is an evolutionary process that changes and evolves era to era. Without Julius Erving, David Thompson, Walter Davis, and Elgin Baylor there never would have been a Michael Jordan. I evolved from them. They presented a challenge, the example I could improve upon. I had the idea that "I have to be better than David Thompson. I have to be better than Julius Erving. I have to be better than Magic Johnson." Those were guiding forces in my development and I used them as motivation.

If I had been born on an island, learned the game all by myself, and developed into the player I became without ever seeing another example, then yes, maybe I would accept being called the greatest. But I have used all the great players who came before me to improve my skills. So I can't be the greatest. It's not fair to diminish them that way. The evolutionary process never ends. Somebody is going to improve upon my game. I don't think I will live to see somebody score 100 points in a game again, but there will be players who evolve and move the game ahead. What could a player do to improve upon my example? They asked the same thing about Elgin Baylor and Dr. J. And that's the beauty of it all. No one knows.

We have seen different aspects of greatness in different bodies. Now we have seen many of those same aspects in one body. I'm certain down the road even more greatness will be seen in a single player. It used to be that great offensive players never played great defense. There was a driving force in me to prove that notion wrong. I proved a great offensive player can play great defense. But somebody will come along who plays even better offense and defense than me. The evolution of greatness doesn't stop with me just as it didn't stop with Baylor, Dr. J, Larry Bird, or Magic. The nature of evolution is to continue. We have all passed something along through our performance and all that has been written.

Somewhere there is a little kid working to enhance what we've done. It may take awhile, but someone will come along who approaches the game the way I did. He won't skip steps. He won't be afraid. He will learn from my example, just as I learned from others. He will master the fundamentals. Maybe he will take off from the free-throw line and do a 360 in midair. Why not? No one thought they would see a 6-foot-9 point guard or a 7-foot-7 center. But here we are. There are now more 6-foot-10 perimeter players than at any time in history. Magic would have been a center 30 years ago. Evolution knows no bounds. Unless they change the height of the basket or otherwise alter the dimensions of the game, there will be a player much greater than me.

I LISTENED, I WAS AWARE OF MY SUCCESS, BUT I NEVER STOPPED TRYING TO GET BETTER.

Long before the late nights and early mornings,

and long before Michael Jordan spent countless hours contemplating his legacy for this book, Bill Huelster had an idea. Mr. Huelster's vision for this project coincided with Rare Air's desire to redefine the standard for visual autobiographical books. Thanks to Mr. Huelster and dozens of others, during the past 12 months opportunity became reality.

From our production partners, all of whom went beyond any reasonable expectation, to Steve Ross and the class act that is Crown Publishers, to our families and friends, the net worth of their contributions is self-evident.

Randy Ginsberg's passion and vision continue to define George Rice & Sons in the print industry. At Potlatch Corporation, Molly Foshay led us through the process of creating a custom proprietary sheet of paper designed to meet our unique print production demands. Like Mr. Ginsberg, Molly's hard work and friendship are forever appreciated.

At BindTech, Dale Nichols showed the power of the entrepreneurial spirit by retooling an entire company to accommodate this project.

At Rare Air, the focus and depth of commitment from Jim Forni and John Vieceli defy expectation. As 100-hour weeks turned into months, the effort, physically and mentally, never dulled. Indeed, they did the work of 10 and no one ever missed the other eight. Their passion is a gift to all those who come in contact with them.

The friendship, support, and love of my wife, Laura, and the blessing that is our daughter, Alexandra, brightened the darkest days and brought comfort to the longest nights. They are my life.

Our collective blessing remains the wonder that is Michael Jordan. Work sessions ran over, photo shoots took much longer than expected, and our demands inevitably extended beyond the parameters of our business model. But the spirit that flows through the corners of Michael's personal life is the same one that defined his professional career. He worked the long hours necessary to bring this project to life despite day-to-day expectations that would have folded a lesser man. Even during the NBA Finals, a time when most would have been consumed by the moment, Michael found peace amid the storm. He opened his house, his life, and his family to all of us despite the blinding glare of celebrity and a late-20th-century culture defined by its desire to deconstruct. Through it all, Michael Jordan showed the world that greatness, true greatness, comes from the inside out. In the end, that's why there will never be another one like him.

Mark Vancil, October, 1998

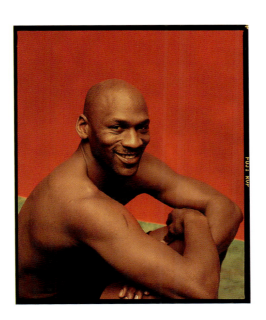

SPECIAL THANKS

At Rare Air
Paul Sheridan, Esq., Christy Egan, Melinda Fry, Seth Guge, Gina Vieceli, Ed Zepernick, Rick Drewes, John Hennessey, and corporate physician, Dr. Terry Sullivan.

At FAME
David Falk, David Bauman, Mary Ellen Nunes, and Estee Portnoy.

At JUMP, Inc.
Jackie Banks, Gus Lett, Clarence Travis, Calvin Holliday, Joe Rokas, Tom West and John Wozniak.

At Crown Publishers
Chip Gibson, Steve Ross, Joan DeMayo, Andy Martin, John Groton, Teresa Nicholas, Hilary Bass, Bruce Harris, Laurie Stark, Debbie Koenig, Jo Fagan, Rebecca Strong, Christian Red, Rich Romano, Amy Boorstein, Florence Porrino, and Mark McCauslin.

At The National Basketball Association
Charlie Rosenzweig, Jan Hubbard, Carmen Romanelli, Nat Butler, Andew Bernstein, Joe Amati, Eric Weinstein, Chris Ekstrand, Mark Broussard, Mark Hale, John Hareas, and Jeanne Tang.

At Brand Jordan/Nike
Howard White, Erin Patton, and Nick Choy.

Others
George Koehler, Liz Silverman, Sharon Powell and Elias Sports Bureau

Compilation Copyright © 1998 by Rare Air, Ltd.
Text Copyright © 1998 by Michael Jordan

Published by Crown Publishers, Inc., 201 East 50th Street, New York, New York 10022. Member of the Crown Publishing Group.

Random House, Inc. New York, Toronto, London, Sydney, Auckland
www.randomhouse.com

CROWN and colophon are trademarks of Crown Publishers, Inc.
Printed in Mexico
Design by Rare Air, Ltd.

Library of Congress Cataloging-in-Publication Data

Jordan, Michael, 1963–
For the love of the game : my story / Michael Jordan. — 1st ed. p. cm.

1. Jordan, Michael, 1963–
2. Basketball players —
United States — Biography.
3. Chicago Bulls (Basketball team)
I. Title.
GV884.J67A28   1998
796.323 '092
[B]—DC21
                    98-8172
                       CIP

ISBN 0-609-60206-3

10 9 8 7 6 5 4 3 2 1

First Edition

PHOTO CREDITS

Andrew D. Bernstein/NBA photos
25,38,40,46-47,50,74-75,76,90,
91,101,131,138-139,152,155,156
Rich Clarkson/Sports Illustrated 43
Scott Cunningham/NBA photos
20,31,150
Corbis 6-7,30
Steve Bonini 37
Nathaniel S. Butler/NBA photos
39,40,42,44,45,46,47,48,49,50,59,
60,63,84,86,90,106-107,122,128,
129,131,132,134,135,144,145,
153,156
Tony Di Zinno 4-5
Sam Forencich/NBA photos
131,142-143
Chris Hamilton/Sports Illustrated
64-65
Mark Hauser 55 (photo courtesy of Bigsby & Kruthers)
Loren Haynes 109
Andy Hayt/NBA photos 123
Walter Iooss, Jr.
1,10,11,26,27,35,36,52-53,61,65,
66-67,68,69,71,77,78-79,80,81,82-
83,86,87,89,90,91,96,97,98,90,102,
103, 114,115,116,117,118-119,121,
136,138,146,147,148,149,154,159
From the Lens of George Kalinsky, Major League Graphics, Inc. 88
Steve Lipofsky/Sports Illustrated 34
John McDonough/Sports Illustrated
29,154-155
Fernando Medina/NBA photos
58,150
Manny Millan/Sports Illustrated
20,50,148-149,154-155
Buck Miller/Sports Illustrated 13
Courtesy of Nike, Inc.
16,17,18,37,124,125
Sandro 9,113,136
Bill Smith 12,13,14,15,20,21,22-23,
24,28, 46,50,51,56-57,62,72-73,85,
90,91,92,93,94,95,99,103, 104-105,
106,108,111,130,131, 132-133,151,
154-155
Pete Stone 110
Bill Sumner 2-3
Cathrine Wessel 140,141
Stephen Wilkes 32-33
Scott Winteron/NBA photos 150